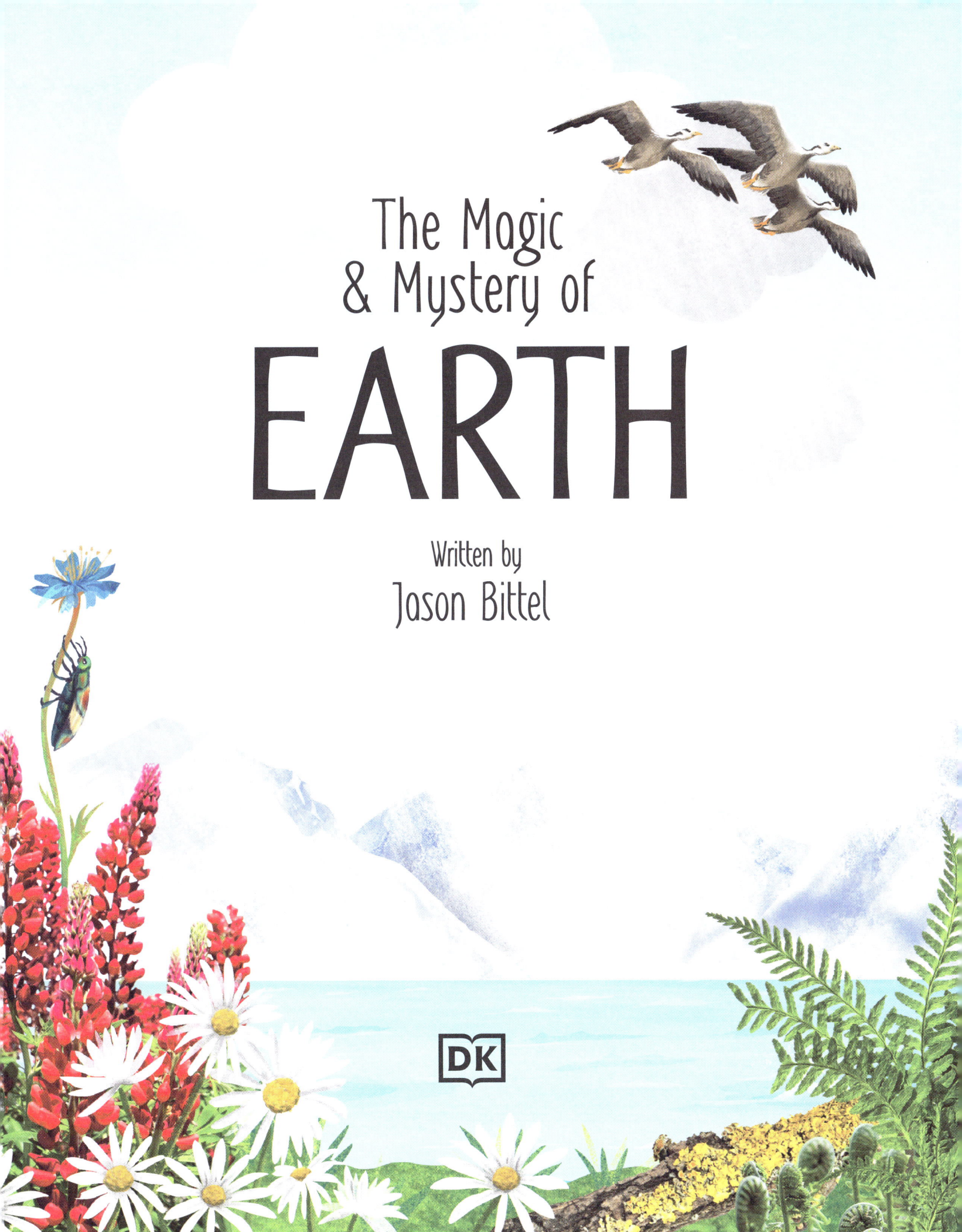

The Magic & Mystery of

EARTH

Written by
Jason Bittel

Author Jason Bittel
Illustrator Claire McElfatrick
Consultant Chris Woodford
Editors Rea Pikula, Lizzie Munsey
Project Art Editor Polly Appleton
Designer Hannah Moore
Production Editor Becky Fallowfield
Senior Production Controller Ena Matagic
Managing Editor Penny Smith
Managing Art Editor Diane Peyton Jones
Art Director Mabel Chan

First published in Great Britain in 2026 by
Dorling Kindersley Limited
20 Vauxhall Bridge Road,
London SW1V 2SA

The authorised representative in the EEA is
Dorling Kindersley Verlag GmbH. Arnulfstr. 124,
80636 Munich, Germany

Copyright © 2026 Dorling Kindersley Limited
A Penguin Random House Company
10 9 8 7 6 5 4 3 2 1
001–352655–Apr/2026

All rights reserved.
No part of this publication may be reproduced, stored in or introduced into a retrieval system, or transmitted, in any form, or by any means (electronic, mechanical, photocopying, recording, or otherwise), without the prior written permission of the copyright owner. DK values and supports copyright. Thank you for respecting intellectual property laws by not reproducing, scanning or distributing any part of this publication by any means without permission. By purchasing an authorised edition, you are supporting writers and artists and enabling DK to continue to publish books that inform and inspire readers.
No part of this publication may be used or reproduced in any manner for the purpose of training artificial intelligence technologies or systems. In accordance with Article 4(3) of the DSM Directive 2019/790, DK expressly reserves this work from the text and data mining exception.

A CIP catalogue record for this book
is available from the British Library.
ISBN: 978-0-2417-7215-7

Printed and bound in China

www.dk.com

INTRODUCTION

From gigantic volcanoes, tangled mangrove forests, and the deep blue sea to tiny pikas, delicate mushrooms, and cheetahs on the prowl, this planet is absolutely bursting with magic and mystery!

It's easy to take these things for granted. We get caught up in our day-to-day lives. We have homework, after-school activities, and chores to do, and sometimes we forget to examine and enjoy the beauty of a cool rock or a breathtaking stream. But once you learn to look for it, you'll find wonder everywhere.

I hope you'll view this book like an adventure as you soar across Earth, its many ecosystems, and even the depths of space beyond. So, are you ready for the journey of a lifetime?

Jason Bittel

CONTENTS

4	**What is Earth?**	42	Grasslands
6	Where are we?	44	Forests
8	Our planet	46	The Arctic
10	Night and day	47	The Antarctic
12	Seasons	48	Mountains
		50	Oceans
14	**Wind and water, land and sea**		
16	The wonder of clouds	52	**Earth and me**
18	Wild weather	54	Planet in danger
20	Moving water	56	Helping the Earth
22	Earth's secret chambers	58	What can I do?
24	Flowing ice		
		60	Glossary
26	**Earth on the move**	62	Index
28	Earth's shifting surface	64	Acknowledgements
30	Earthquakes		
32	Fiery features		
34	Recycled rocks		

36 **Life on Earth**
38 Living things
40 Deserts

WHAT IS EARTH?

There are many ways to describe this giant ball of rock in space: an ocean planet, a source of life, a home.

Water blankets 70 per cent of Earth's surface, while the rest of the planet is made of solid ground. Of the eight planets in our Solar System, Earth is the only place we know where life exists. This isn't an accident; Earth has a special, just-right mix of factors that help it teem with life.

Simply put, scientists have yet to find anything like Earth. This planet is extremely special, and we must protect it.

Ocean planet
From space, Earth's most obvious feature is its blue oceans.

Where are we?

For most of recorded history, people thought Earth was the centre of the Universe. Now we know that this planet is just one tiny speck flying through the colossal expanse of space. It's a speck we're lucky to have!

Earth is the only place we know of that supports life. This is thanks to a combination of liquid water, an element known as oxygen, and just the right amount of sunlight.

Our Solar System is about 4.6 billion years old. As well as its eight planets, the Solar System contains five dwarf planets including Pluto, hundreds of moons, and other space objects, such as comets and asteroids.

EARTH

The English word "earth" means "soil" or "ground". But this is not the only name for our planet. For example, in French it's called *Terre*, and in Indonesian it's known as *Bumi*.

THE SOLAR SYSTEM

Earth is one of eight planets located in a part of space called the Solar System. At the centre of our Solar System is a star called the Sun, and each planet travels around the Sun on its own path, which is called its orbit.

The Milky Way has a bar of stars at its centre, with two main arms spiralling out from it.

The Universe is thought to be around 92 billion light years across, and still growing. (A light year is the distance light can travel in one year.) It's getting bigger even as you read this book!

OUR SOLAR SYSTEM

THE MILKY WAY

THE MILKY WAY

A galaxy is a collection of billions of stars and their solar systems. Our Solar System is part of a spiral-shaped galaxy called the Milky Way. It's named this for the way it can make the sky look hazy on a clear, dark night.

THE UNIVERSE

The Universe is everything that exists, including around 200 billion galaxies. The Milky Way with its billions of stars is just one of these galaxies.

Our planet

Earth is not just a giant ball of rock – it's actually a complex structure made of many layers. This includes the atmosphere: a mixture of gases that surrounds Earth.

CRUST
Earth's crust is where we live. It's Earth's thinnest layer, made of solid rock.

EARTH'S LAYERS
When Earth formed about 4.5 billion years ago, its heaviest metals sank towards the centre, while lighter materials stayed nearer to the surface. This process gave Earth its layers.

You'd need a spacesuit to

10 km (6 miles)

Weather balloons collect information from the troposphere.

INNER CORE
This dense sphere of solid iron and nickel metal is nearly as hot as the surface of the Sun.

OUTER CORE
The outer core is also mostly made up of iron and nickel, but here they are liquid, not solid.

MANTLE
The mantle contains semi-solid iron, magnesium, and silicon. It is thought to be as thick as caramel.

TROPOSPHERE
The troposphere stretches from the ground all the way up to the tops of mountains and even most clouds.

Even the

travel up to the mesosphere or beyond!

10,000 km (6,200 miles)

600 km (375 miles)

85 km (53 miles)

50 km (31 miles)

EARTH'S ATMOSPHERE

Earth's atmosphere is made up of nitrogen, oxygen, and a mixture of other gases. It gives us the air we breathe and protects us from some of the harmful rays produced by the Sun.

The International Space Station orbits Earth in this layer.

As meteors burn up, they produce streaks of light we can see in the sky.

Auroras are dazzling, dancing lights in the sky, which usually occur in the thermosphere.

Satellites in the exosphere have an excellent view of Earth.

This calm layer of the atmosphere is perfect for smooth flights.

STRATOSPHERE
The stratosphere contains the ozone layer, a thin shell of gases that helps shield Earth from the Sun.

MESOSPHERE
This is the coldest layer of the atmosphere. Most meteors (space rocks) burn up as they travel through here.

THERMOSPHERE
This is the thickest layer of the atmosphere. It absorbs harmful ultraviolet radiation and X-rays from the Sun.

EXOSPHERE
This is the last layer of atmosphere before airless space begins. The air is very thin here.

deepest-drilled holes reach nowhere **near** Earth's core.

IN AND OUT OF LIGHT

Earth travels in a loop (orbit) around the Sun, spinning as it goes. As it spins, the half of the planet that faces the Sun's light gets daytime. At the same time, the parts of Earth that face the darkness of space experience night.

24 hours
One day is 24 hours, because that's how long it takes Earth to make a complete turn on its axis.

Earth's axis

Earth

Earth spins on a slightly tilted axis (an imaginary line through Earth's centre). This causes different parts to be closer to the Sun at different times of year.

Direction of spin

North Pole

Night and day

Both the Ancient Greeks and Chinese believed the Sun was carried across the sky each day in a fiery chariot. Now we know that's not the case: night and day come from Earth spinning around on its axis.

South Pole

Earth's poles can sometimes be completely light or dark for months at a time.

365 days
One year is 365 days, because that's how long it takes Earth to complete one full journey around the Sun.

The Sun

Day

Night

Earth's movement

Blocking the Sun
The Moon travels around Earth. If it crosses in front of the Sun it can briefly block the Sun's light, causing a solar eclipse.

If it's day where you are, it will usually be night on the other side of the world.

Crossing the sky
From Earth, it can look like the Sun is moving across the sky over the course of a day. However, it's really Earth that is rotating!

Seasons

Earth moves around the Sun at a tilt, which means that parts of the planet receive more sunlight and warmth at some times of the year than at others. This gives us our seasons. Seasons are stronger further away from the equator (an imaginary circle around Earth's middle).

AUTUMN

Autumn comes between summer and winter. Days get shorter and the weather becomes cooler because there's less sunlight. Some plants prepare for the cold by changing the colour of their leaves and allowing them to drop off.

WINTER

Winter comes when days are at their shortest. It is the coldest season, and often brings snow and ice. Food becomes more scarce. To survive, many animals will migrate to other areas, or go into hibernation (a sleep-like state).

Monsoons
Many tropical areas have just two seasons: one dry and one wet. The wet season can be extremely wet and windy. This is called a monsoon.

SPRING

As Earth's tilt reverses, days become longer again, it becomes warmer, and both plants and hibernating animals wake up. Spring is when many flowers bloom, and animals lay their eggs or give birth to their young.

SUMMER

The longest days of the year are in summer. All the extra sunshine also makes this the hottest season. Plants use the energy from sunlight to grow, and many use that energy boost to begin making fruit.

Clouds or UFOs?
These clouds form when wet air rises over mountains. They are sometimes mistaken for UFOs (Unidentified Flying Objects) because of their rounded, saucer-like shape.

WIND AND WATER, LAND AND SEA

Earth is like a work of art. It is covered in a patchwork of sparkling waters and rolling landscapes, with more wonders hidden beneath the surface.

Water is the liquid that makes life happen. It exists in a constant cycle, with freshwater and saltwater moving and changing from clouds to rivers to sea. Winds blow around the planet, carrying water with them.

The movement of water shapes the land around it. Icy glaciers carve into mountainsides, rivers wear away at plains, and rainwater slowly turns hollows into caves.

The wonder of clouds

There are many different types of cloud, from fluffy, white clouds on a clear day to dark thunderclouds in a storm. Clouds are probably more important than you realize – they are full of water and help keep our planet cool.

What is a cloud?
Clouds are collections of tiny droplets of water or ice crystals. They form when warm air rises and cools, and the water vapour it holds condenses into liquid water or ice around tiny particles of dust, dirt, or smoke in the air.

Falling from the sky
Tiny drops of water and ice bump together inside clouds, getting bigger and bigger. Eventually, they become too heavy to float. At this point, they fall down to Earth as rain, snow, or hail, which are all known as precipitation.

Rain
Liquid water precipitation is called rain. It can vary in size, from tiny sprinkles up to heavy drips.

Snow
In freezing temperatures, ice crystals form inside clouds. They float down to the ground as snow.

Sleet
The slushy wet mixture known as sleet is formed when snow melts as it falls to the ground.

Hail
Hailstones are balls of solid ice. They range from pea-sized to bigger than a golf ball!

CUMULONIMBUS
These tall, dense, and dark clouds are often called thunderstorm clouds. This is because they are the only cloud type to consistently make lightning, thunder, and hail. Sometimes, they can even bring tornadoes.

CIRROCUMULUS
These high, thin clouds are mostly made of ice crystals. They can look like a patchy layer stretched across the sky.

CIRRUS
Soft, silky, and less solid-looking than cirrocumulus, cirrus clouds are usually see-through.

CIRROSTRATUS
Cirrostratus clouds can blanket the sky with a thin curtain of white.

High-level clouds — Above 6,000 m (20,000 ft)

CLOUD TYPES
Scientists have grouped clouds into 10 basic types, with names based on how high they are or that hint at their appearance. For example, the word "cirrus" comes from the Latin word for "curl".

NIMBOSTRATUS
These are dark, grey clouds caused by falling rain or snow. They are so thick that they can make the Sun disappear.

ALTOCUMULUS
These common clouds appear as many little clumps, also known as cloudlets.

ALTOSTRATUS
These clouds form a thick sheet but the Sun can still shine through. They are thicker than cirrostratus.

Mid-level clouds — 2,000–6,000 m (6,500–20,000 ft)

STRATOCULUMUS
These clouds are lumpy and rounded, and can look a bit like honeycomb.

CUMULUS
These fluffy, dense pillows can shine bright white on a sunny day.

STRATUS
Stratus clouds can mean rain, but they can also break up to reveal a bright blue sky.

Low-level clouds — Below 2,000 m (6,500 ft)

THUNDERSTORMS

Thunderstorms bring wind, rain, flashes of lightning, and rumbles of thunder. These storms are most common in spring and summer, when warm, humid air rises and meets cold air. Around 16 million thunderstorms happen every year.

Thunder and lightning
Lightning is a zap of light caused by charges building up inside a storm cloud. It makes a rumbling sound, called thunder. We see lightning before we hear thunder, because light travels much faster than sound.

Wild weather

Most weather, such as wind and rain, is a normal part of life on Earth. However, sometimes weather can push into the extremes. Each kind of extreme weather brings different risks. Being aware can help keep you safe!

HEATWAVES

When temperatures rise higher than usual and stay that way for two or more days, you've got a heatwave. This may not sound very extreme, but heatwaves are a deadly form of extreme weather. In the USA, they kill more people than any other form of extreme weather.

The heatwave of 2003
In 2003, a heatwave in Europe led to droughts, forest fires, and many deaths. It was thought to be the worst heatwave for 500 years.

HURRICANES

Tropical storms are swirling winds that form over warm oceans. Once a tropical storm's wind speed reaches 119 kph (74 mph), it officially becomes a hurricane. Hurricanes are dangerous, with destructive winds and ocean surges.

Changing names
Hurricanes are known as different things in different parts of the world. They are "hurricanes" in the North Atlantic and Northeast Pacific oceans, "typhoons" in the West Pacific, and "cyclones" in the Indian Ocean and Australia.

TORNADOES

Tornadoes are narrow funnels of rapidly spinning air that reach from a storm cloud to the ground. Small tornadoes last for only minutes and do little damage. Larger tornadoes can last for hours and rip up buildings and trees as they move across the landscape.

Super speeds
Some tornadoes move very quickly, reaching speeds of up to 120 kph (75 mph). The spinning winds inside them can top 500 kph (310 mph).

Moving water

Water is everywhere, even in the air around us and hidden below our feet. It doesn't stay still, but constantly moves and changes in a process known as the water cycle.

Transpiration
Plants release water vapour through their leaves and into the sky. This is called transpiration.

Condensation
When water vapour cools, it changes back into a liquid. This is known as condensation, and is one way clouds form.

Evaporation
Heat from the Sun warms liquid water, turning it into a gas called water vapour. This is known as evaporation.

Less than three per cent of all water on Earth is freshwater. The rest is found in the oceans, and is much too salty to drink.

Precipitation
When the water droplets or ice crystals inside clouds become heavy enough, they fall out of the sky as rain, snow, or hail. This is precipitation.

Glaciers
Some parts of the water cycle move more slowly than others. Glaciers are slow-moving chunks of ice that can trap water for millions of years!

Lakes
Lakes are bodies of water that are almost completely surrounded by land.

Rivers
The water from rain, snow, or hail flows into rivers and lakes, which carry it downhill to the ocean. Some rivers are small and flow fast, while others are wide and slow.

Groundwater
Around one-third of all Earth's freshwater is hidden away underground. This is known as groundwater, and it feeds rivers, lakes, and oceans.

Ocean
The ocean is a gigantic body of saltwater that holds 97 per cent of all of Earth's water.

Earth's secret chambers

Caves are underground holes, or chambers. They come in a range of shapes and sizes, and can form in a few different ways. Some of these hidden worlds are full of interesting rock formations and wildlife!

Limestone caves
Caves often form when limestone rock in the ground is slowly broken down by water. These are one of the most common kinds of cave.

Stalactite

Column

Stalactites and stalagmites
When water full of minerals drips through a cave, it can form icicle-like stalactites on the ceiling and pillar-like stalagmites on the cave floor. These can join up to create columns.

Stalagmite

Cave orb-weaver spider

THE LIFE OF A CAVE
It can take thousands or even millions of years for caves to form. Here is one way it can happen in limestone.

ROCK WEAKENS
Tiny cracks get larger over time as water flows, freezes, and wears away at the rock.

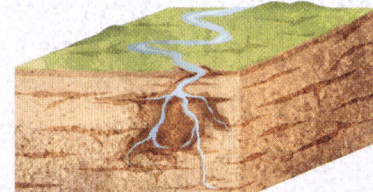

BIGGER CRACKS
As time passes, the water can carve out bigger crevices in the rock.

ROOF COLLAPSES
Eventually, the hollow can become so large that the roof above it falls in, leading to large underground spaces.

Bats

Echolocation
Bats listen to echoes to help them find their way around in total darkness.

Living in the dark
Some animals have developed powerful senses that help them live in dark caves. These animals are known as troglofauna.

Blind cave fish

Crickets

Cave millipede

TYPES OF CAVE
Caves don't just form in limestone. Here are two other ways they appear, each creating a unique underground world.

ICE CAVES
As glaciers melt, the flowing water can cut channels into the ice. Hot vents in the ground can also melt ice sheets to create ice caves.

LAVA TUBES
These tubes are underground passageways created when some lava cools but the rest drains away, leaving an empty tunnel behind.

Flowing ice

Have you ever heard someone call a glacier a "river of ice"? Well, it's true! Glaciers are giant masses of ice and snow, squished down and packed tight. Glaciers move, though very slowly – they usually travel just a few centimetres per day.

An icy river

Glaciers move because they are very heavy. Their weight makes them creep down mountainsides and valleys. As they move, glaciers pick up dirt, rocks, and even boulders.

Glaciers flowing between high, rocky mountains are called **valley glaciers**.

Glaciers form when snow falls then gets **squashed together**, becoming large, flowing ice.

Streaks of dirt and grit show where different glaciers have joined.

Unlike ice cubes, glaciers are not smooth – they are covered in **cracks**.

The place where a glacier ends is known as the **terminus**.

Big cracks in the ice are called **crevasses**.

Where ice from the glacier melts, the water **pools** at the bottom then **flows away** downhill.

Glaciers, icecaps, and permanent snow hold almost 70 per cent of all of Earth's freshwater.

When glaciers **meet** they can flow together, becoming a larger glacier.

After the ice
Glaciers have a huge impact on the land they scrape across. They carve the ground into new shapes, and leave behind a new pattern of lakes and rivers.

When glaciers meet they can shape mountains into **sharp ridges**.

Glaciers carve valleys into **U-shapes** as they flow through them.

Melted glaciers can leave behind **rivers** and long, narrow **lakes**.

Glaciers carve **hollows** in the land that fill with water when they melt.

Glaciers often drop off huge chunks of **rock** that they once carried along.

As they melt, glaciers can leave behind piles of soil and rock called **moraines**.

25

Fairy chimneys
These rock formations in Cappadocia, Turkey, emerged when volcanic eruptions rained ash over the region. This hardened into rock, which, over time, the weather sculpted into these pillars.

EARTH ON THE MOVE

Rocks seem so permanent. Even the most ordinary stones around you might be billions of years old. But rocks are constantly changing.

Earth's crust is made of gigantic layers of rock, known as tectonic plates. Though you can't see them, they move too, carrying whole continents with them and slowly remaking Earth's surface in the process. Where these plates meet, they can unleash some of nature's most powerful events: earthquakes and volcanoes.

Earth's shifting surface

Earth's surface isn't as solid as it looks. It is made up of huge, slowly moving pieces, which are even bigger than the continents that sit on top of them.

TECTONIC PLATES
The pieces of Earth's surface are known as tectonic plates. There are seven large plates and several more small ones.

Tectonic activity
When plates move and push against each other, they can cause earthquakes and volcanic eruptions.

EURASIAN PLATE
AFRICAN PLATE
INDO-AUSTRALIAN PLATE
ANTARCTIC PLATE

Plate boundaries
The places where tectonic plates meet are called plate boundaries. The edges of the plates meet in three different ways.

Moving together
When plates collide they can create new mountain ranges or deep-sea trenches.

Sliding past
Plates that slide past each other can make the ground shake, causing earthquakes.

Pulling apart
When plates pull apart earthquakes may happen. Melted rock can also rise up and cool between the plates, forming volcanoes.

Deep Earth energy
Plates move because of heat energy inside Earth. Movements below the crust lift and shift the plates above them.

LAND ON THE MOVE
Over the course of millions of years, Earth's plates have moved so much that the continents were in very different positions from where they are today.

Pangaea
Around 250 million years ago, there was only one continent, called Pangaea, and one ocean called Panthalassa.

NORTH AMERICAN PLATE

Tectonic plates move at about the same speed your fingernails grow.

Ring of Fire

SOUTH AMERICAN PLATE

PACIFIC PLATE

Two continents
Around 200 million years ago during the Triassic Period, Pangaea broke into two continents: Laurasia and Gondwana.

Present day
The continents we know have been in place for about 65 million years.

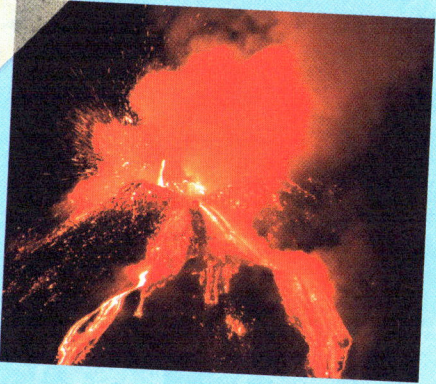

RING OF FIRE
Around 90 per cent of Earth's earthquakes and 75 per cent of its volcanoes occur around the Pacific Plate. It's known as the Ring of Fire!

Earthquakes

When tectonic plates move past one another they can get stuck. This causes pressure to build up. Eventually the plates move and this energy is released, surging outwards from its source and shaking the ground above. This energy movement is known as an earthquake.

7+
This magnitude of earthquake can be very dangerous. Anything above 7 is thought of as a major earthquake.

4–6
An earthquake measuring 4 to 6 might cause slight damage to buildings and other structures.

1–3
At 1, 2, or 3 an earthquake is large enough to be recorded by scientists, but small enough that people won't usually feel it.

MEASURING QUAKES

The power of an earthquake is measured by a system known as moment magnitude. The higher the number, the more powerful the earthquake.

Fault line
An earthquake happens at a fault line (a crack in Earth's crust), where tectonic plates meet.

Epicentre
The epicentre is the place on Earth's surface directly above the focus. This is where the shaking is felt the strongest.

Focus
The focus is the place inside Earth where energy is released and the earthquake actually begins.

Earthquake-proof design
In areas where earthquakes happen often the buildings are designed to be stronger and more flexible, to absorb the shaking.

Scientists detect around 20,000 earthquakes each year, but most can't be felt by people.

Seismic waves
These are waves of energy, which we feel as shakes. They travel away from the earthquake's focus and through Earth, like ripples on a pond.

Destruction
Serious earthquakes can cause damage to buildings, roads, and power lines, and even create landslides.

Giant sea waves
When earthquakes happen underneath the ocean, they sometimes create huge waves known as tsunamis. Tsunamis can travel great distances and get larger before they reach the shore. They can be very dangerous.

Fiery features

Volcanoes, hot springs, geysers, and fumaroles all exist because of molten-hot volcanic activity inside Earth. Are you ready to get fired up?

Volcanic ash
During an eruption, a volcano can send ash as high as Earth's stratosphere.

Volcanic gases
Volcanoes can release steam, carbon dioxide, sulphur dioxide, and other gases that make the air dangerous to breathe. This can harm plants and animals.

BLAST FROM BELOW
Volcanoes are openings in the ground where melted rock (magma) can move from inside Earth to above its surface.

Magma or lava?
Melted rock inside Earth is called magma. Once it reaches the surface, it is known as lava.

ERUPTION!
Lava, gas, ash, and solid rocks can explode out of volcanoes. This is called an eruption. Lava can burst out, or it can slowly flow over the land, burying everything in its path.

HOT SPRINGS

When water is heated up by magma below Earth's surface, it can become a hot spring. Hot springs are often beautiful but they can also be extremely hot and full of dangerous chemicals.

Colourful spring
Grand Prismatic Spring in Yellowstone, USA, contains tiny creatures called thermophiles, which give it vibrant colours.

GEYSERS

When magma heats channels of underground water, some of that water can eventually become steam. The steam expands, and rockets the rest of the water up to the surface and into the air as a geyser.

The Strokkur geyser
This geyser in Iceland erupts every 4 to 10 minutes. It can launch superheated water up to 40 m (130 ft) into the air.

FUMAROLES

These vents are found near active volcanoes. They are cracks in Earth's surface that allow hot steam and volcanic gases to escape into the air.

Sulphurous vent
A fumarole that gives out lots of a yellow-coloured chemical, called sulphur, is sometimes called a solfatara.

Recycled rocks

Rocks may all look similar, but there are actually three basic types: metamorphic, igneous, and sedimentary. Over time rocks can change from one type to another in a process known as the rock cycle. Here is how it works.

Cooling
When magma erupts from Earth as lava, it cools down, becoming a solid rock. Magma can also cool and slowly harden underground.

Igneous
These rocks form when melted rock solidifies, which can happen either above or under ground.

Basalt

Marble

Metamorphic
When sedimentary rock is put under extreme heat and pressure inside Earth, it can change into metamorphic rock.

Melting
When rock gets hot enough it melts to form magma. Magma that makes it to Earth's surface is called lava.

ROCK FORMATIONS

The rock cycle has created amazing formations and landscapes all over the world. No two are the same, and they are still being shaped to this day.

Zhangye National Geopark
These hills in China aren't painted! They were created by movements in Earth's crust, followed by millions of years of sedimentary rock being worn away.

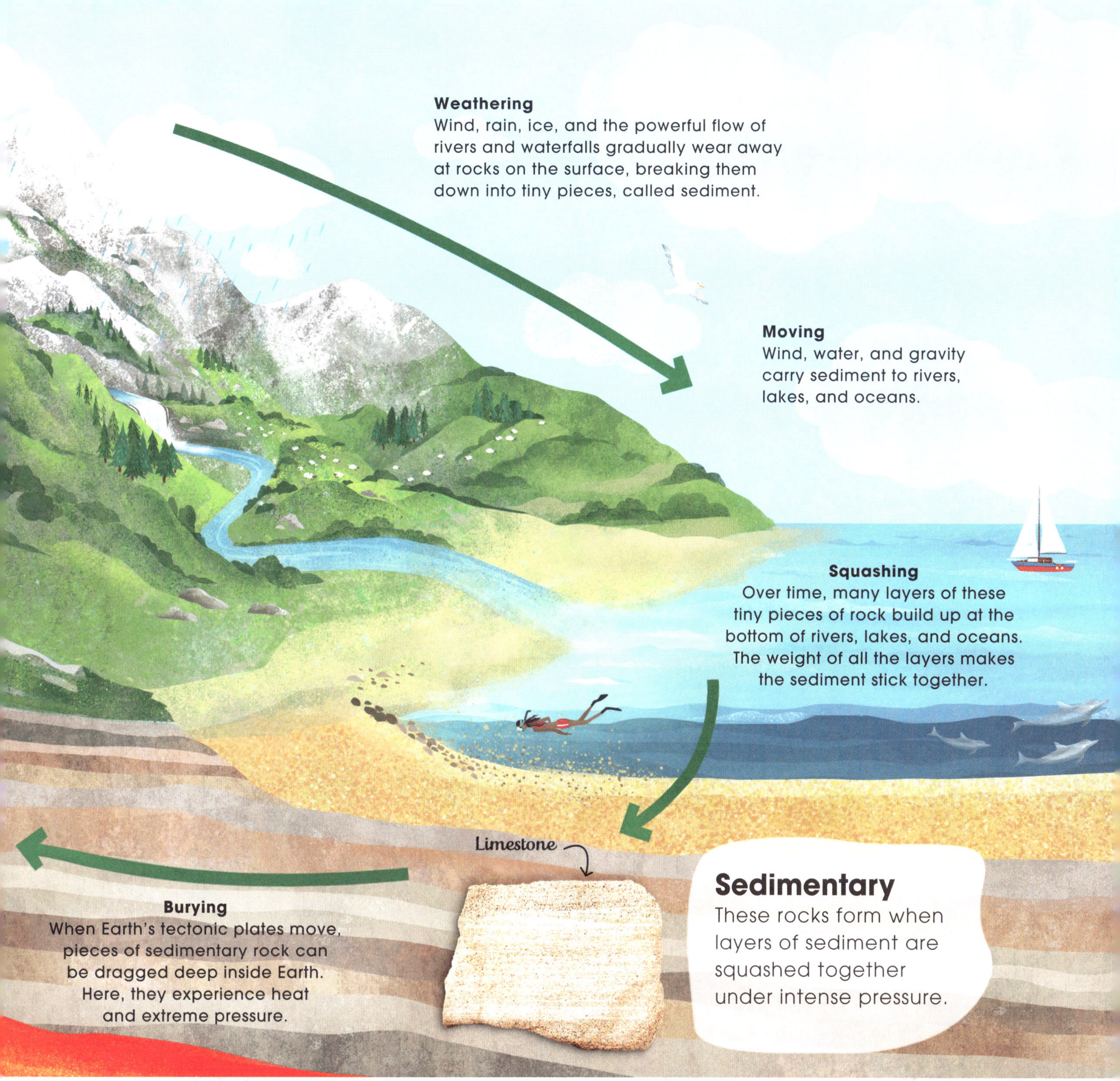

Weathering
Wind, rain, ice, and the powerful flow of rivers and waterfalls gradually wear away at rocks on the surface, breaking them down into tiny pieces, called sediment.

Moving
Wind, water, and gravity carry sediment to rivers, lakes, and oceans.

Squashing
Over time, many layers of these tiny pieces of rock build up at the bottom of rivers, lakes, and oceans. The weight of all the layers makes the sediment stick together.

Limestone

Sedimentary
These rocks form when layers of sediment are squashed together under intense pressure.

Burying
When Earth's tectonic plates move, pieces of sedimentary rock can be dragged deep inside Earth. Here, they experience heat and extreme pressure.

The Grand Canyon's Inner Gorge
The metamorphic and igneous rocks at the bottom of the Grand Canyon in the USA may be 1.8 billion years old.

Giant's Causeway
This group of more than 40,000 basalt columns in Northern Ireland were created by volcanic eruptions, and not by a giant, as legends say!

Slow but hidden
Sloths move slowly, which allows tiny algae to grow on their fur. This makes them harder for predators to spot.

LIFE ON EARTH

Scientists believe life first squirmed into existence about 3.7 billion years ago.

What's more, life on Earth nearly died out not once, but five separate times, during what are known as mass extinction events. Today, scientists estimate that there are roughly 8.7 million species of living things on this planet, and there are more that have yet to be discovered!

From tiny termites in grasslands and towering trees in hot, steamy rainforests to resilient polar bears in the icy cold Arctic, living things are found in all sorts of habitats, all over Earth.

Whip spider

Orangutan

Living things

Scientists organize living things into categories. Some of the biggest ones are animals, plants, and fungi. These categories are then divided into smaller groups. For example, the animals group includes invertebrates, reptiles, mammals, fish, birds, and amphibians.

Octopus

Chameleon

Reptiles
The reptile group includes crocodiles, snakes, and lizards. They are cold-blooded, which means they rely on the Sun for warmth, and have scaly or armour-like skin.

Mammals
All mammals are warm-blooded and feed their babies milk. Most are covered in hair or fur. This animal group includes humans and pets, such as dogs.

Jewel beetle

Invertebrates
This group has one thing in common: no backbone. It includes a huge range of animals, from insects to octopuses.

Komodo dragon

Galápagos tortoise

Kangaroos

Otter

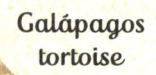
Lupins

PLANTS
Plants make their own food by turning sunlight into energy, and in the process give us oxygen to breathe. The plant category is split into two main groups: plants that produce flowers and plants that don't.

Ferns

Daisies

Mosses

ANIMALS

Animals breathe, move, communicate, and sense the world around them. They get the energy they need by eating plants and each other. Most animals are invertebrates, and the rest of the animal kingdom are vertebrates (animals with a backbone).

Northern cardinal

Is it alive?
All living things have a few things in common:
- Movement
- Growth
- Reproduction
- Sensing and responding to their surroundings
- Taking in energy
- Getting rid of waste

Seahorse

Ostrich

Axolotl

Salmon

Fish
These animals live in water and usually breathe through organs called gills. Most fish are covered in a layer of protective scales.

Birds
Birds have light bones, wings, and feathers to help them fly. Most birds can fly, but some such as ostriches are flightless.

Amphibians
These animals spend most of their lives in or near water, sometimes moving onto land. They are cold-blooded and most lay eggs.

Manta ray

Fire salamander

Peacock

Paradoxical frog

FUNGI
These are not plants or animals, but their own special group, which includes mushrooms and moulds. They feed on dead or rotting plants and animals.

Veiled lady

Orange peel fungus

Deserts

There are a few types of desert, which all have one thing in common: they receive little rain. The Mojave Desert in the USA is an example of a hot and dry desert. All sorts of plants and animals can be found here, despite the lack of water.

Joshua trees

Greater roadrunner

Creosote bush

Saving water
Most desert plants have small leaves, so they lose as little water through them as possible.

Black-tailed jackrabbits

Desert tortoise

Most deserts receive less than 25 cm (10 in) of rain a year.

Mountain lion

Burrowing owls

Gila monster

It's cooler underground
Many desert animals spend the daytime under rocks, or in burrows underground. It's much cooler down there!

Desert camouflage
Animals that live in deserts are often brown or red. These colours allow them to hide among sand and rocks.

Giant desert hairy scorpion

Semiarid
These deserts are hot and dry during the summer, but usually receive some rain in the winter. This makes them wetter than places such as the Mojave Desert.

Coastal
Some deserts are next to the ocean. Fog blows in from the ocean, bringing water to the plants and animals that live there, but they get little actual rain.

Cold
Antarctica is covered in frozen water, but it gets very little rain or snow. It's the largest desert on the planet!

Grasslands

Grasslands are open, flat areas where most of the plants are grasses. This isn't like the grass in a garden – some grasses can be 3 m (10 ft) tall! The grassland shown here is savanna in Africa.

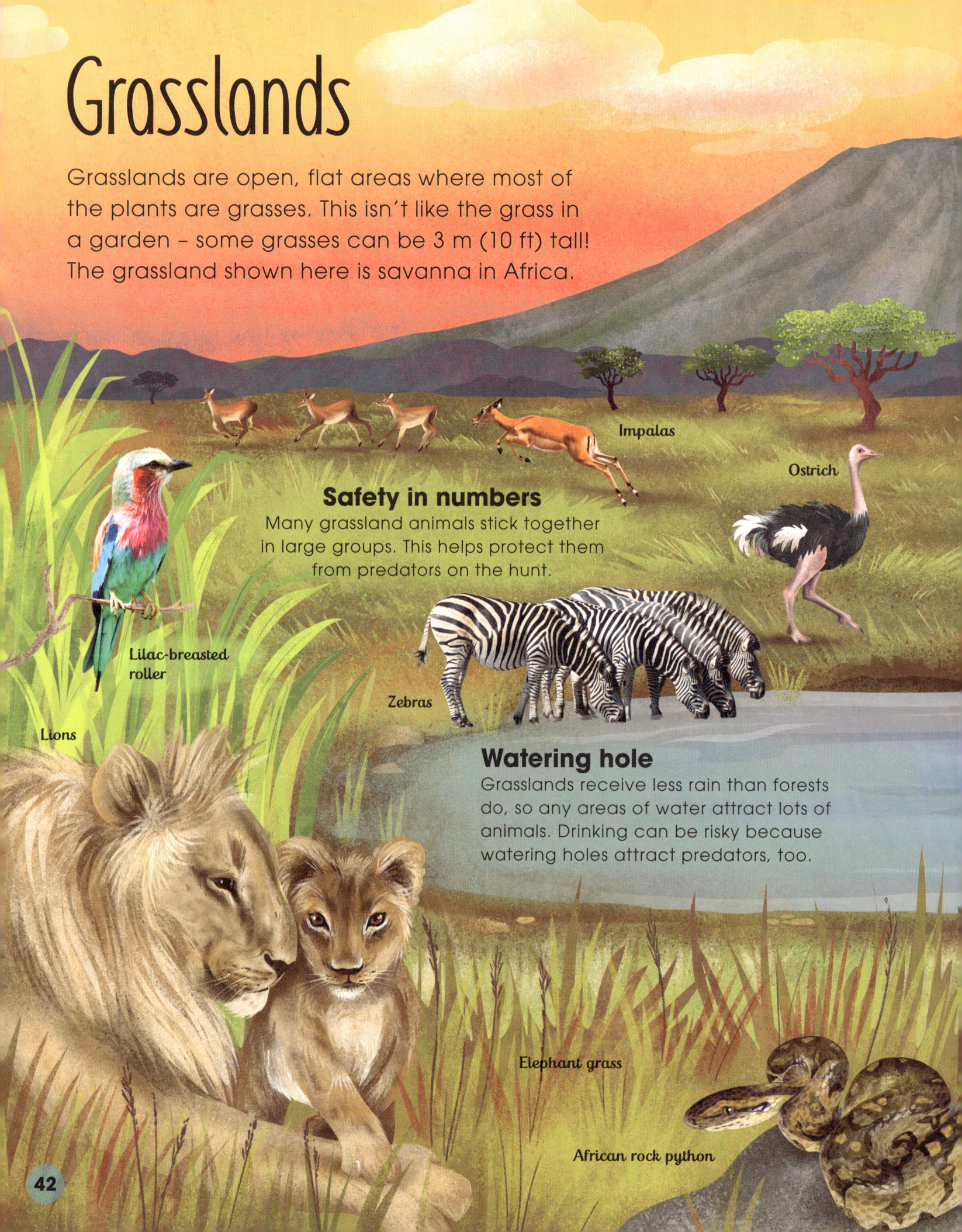

Impalas

Ostrich

Safety in numbers
Many grassland animals stick together in large groups. This helps protect them from predators on the hunt.

Lilac-breasted roller

Zebras

Lions

Watering hole
Grasslands receive less rain than forests do, so any areas of water attract lots of animals. Drinking can be risky because watering holes attract predators, too.

Elephant grass

African rock python

White-backed vultures

Tough hunting
Predators spend much of their time hunting, but most hunts end in failure. Predators must work hard to survive.

Acacia trees

Cheetah

Giraffe

Towering nest
Termites are tiny, wood-eating insects. But the nests they build can be huge, towering up to 5 m (16 ft) above the savanna.

African bush elephants

Savanna termites

Grey crowned crane

Forests

Welcome to the kingdom of trees! Forests are home to a huge range of plants and animals, but the most common living things there are *actually* trees. Forests vary depending on the temperature of the area.

Harpy eagle

Sloth

Black spider monkey

Tree life
Black spider monkeys swing through the tall trees, squealing and barking to communicate with each other.

Jaguar

Capybaras

Poison dart frog

Hands off
The bright colours of a poison dart frog warn predators that taking a bite could be deadly.

Pink river dolphin

Freshwater giant
The pink river dolphin can weigh up to 160 kg (350 lb)!

TROPICAL

Also known as rainforests, tropical forests are usually found near the equator, where it's warm and wet. The year-round wet weather helps the trees grow thick and tall.

TEMPERATE

Temperate forests usually experience all four seasons each year. Unlike tropical and boreal forests, they are neither too hot nor too cold.

BOREAL

In cold areas near the North Pole there are boreal forests. They usually have lots of conifer trees, such as pines.

The Arctic

The northernmost region on Earth is the Arctic. It has mostly open ocean and sea ice, and includes the northern tips of North America, Asia, and Europe.

Arctic tern

Two summers
To enjoy summers around the globe, Arctic terns make the longest journey of any animal, flying from the Arctic to Antarctica.

The Arctic ↘

Arctic wolves

Reindeer

Arctic hare

Beluga whales

Polar bear

Blending in
Many Arctic animals, such as hares and rock ptarmigan, change the colour of their fur or feathers from brown in the summer to white in the winter to blend in with their surroundings.

Walruses

Built for winter
Walruses and other marine mammals have thick layers of fat called blubber, which help them stay warm in icy Arctic waters.

Narwhal

Least weasel

Treeless plains
The Arctic tundra is an area of flat plains with no trees. In winter it is covered in snow and ice and the soil is frozen. In summer, the soil thaws and a few plants grow.

Rock ptarmigan

Special skill
Least weasels are one of the smallest predators. They are tiny enough to be able to hunt for food all around the Arctic.

The Antarctic

Antarctica is a continent located at the southernmost part of the planet. It is covered almost completely in ice, and is the coldest, driest, and windiest place on Earth.

When it's winter in the Arctic, it's summer in Antarctica.

Wandering albatross

Icy survivor
Only a handful of plants can survive in Antarctica. The Antarctic pearlwort is one of them, and has tiny flowers in the summer.

Safety in numbers
Emperor penguins huddle together in big groups to block the wind and share body heat. They take turns spending time in the cosy middle!

Antarctic pearlwort

Emperor penguins

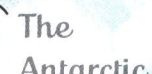
The Antarctic

Antarctic blue whale

Adélie penguins

Feeding the Antarctic
Krill are tiny ocean creatures. They are eaten by a large number of Antarctic animals, from fish and penguins to gigantic whales.

Under the sea
Antarctica has six types of seal. They spend a lot of their time underwater, hunting for food.

Weddell seal

47

Mountains

Towering mountains form when tectonic plates crash into each other, pushing land upwards over millions of years. Many different kinds of plants and animals have adapted to survive at the very top of the world.

Andean condor

On the hunt
Mountain lions are top predators found all the way from Canada to Chile.

Mountain lion

MOUNT ACONCAGUA
This mountain in Argentina is part of the Andes mountain range, which runs across South America.

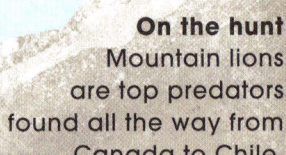

Guanacos

Alien cushion
Mounds of yareta look like green blobs, but they are actually groups of tiny plants.

Golden eagle

Beating the cold
Guanacos have two layers of super-soft fur. It protects them from freezing temperatures in the Andean highlands.

Yareta

MATTERHORN
Famous for its pyramid shape, the Matterhorn is a peak in the Alps that straddles Switzerland and Italy.

Alpine ibex

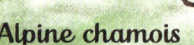

Alpine chamois

Swiss pine

Apollo butterflies

Eye see you
Red eyespots on the hindwings of this butterfly may scare predators away.

Alpine marmot

Expert digger
The marmot's underground burrow helps protect it from predators and harsh weather.

MOUNT EVEREST

Part of the Himalayas mountain range in Asia, Mount Everest is the tallest mountain on Earth.

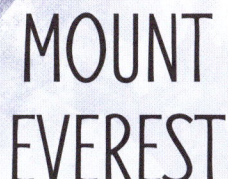
Bar-headed geese

Snow leopard

High in the sky
This spider lives higher up than any other spider on Earth!

Himalayan jumping spider

Rare in nature
The vivid blue of these petals is very unusual for a natural flower.

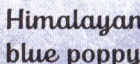
Himalayan blue poppy

Large-eared pika

Summer harvesters
Pikas are related to rabbits. They dry flowers in the Sun, then store them in burrows to eat over the winter.

MOUNT ELBERT

Mount Elbert in Colorado, USA is the highest peak in the Rocky Mountains.

White-tailed ptarmigan

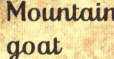
Mountain goat

In full bloom
This slow-growing plant doesn't flower until it's 10–20 years old.

Get a grip
Mountain goats have special grips on their hooves that help them climb dangerous terrain.

Old man of the mountain

Bighorn sheep

Blue whale

Oceans

The ocean holds more living things than any other place on Earth! It has a range of different habitats, from coastal wetlands and kelp forests to coral reefs, the open ocean, and the deep sea.

Here be giants
The open ocean is home to Earth's giants. The blue whale is not just the largest animal on Earth, it is also the largest animal to have ever lived.

Whale sharks are the **biggest fish in the ocean,** growing up to nearly 19 m (62 ft).

Pilot fish swim closely to whale sharks, **cleaning their skin** and hiding from predators.

Pilot fish

Whale shark

DEEP SEA
At the bottom of the ocean there is no light, and the pressure of water pushing down from above is enormous. The animals that live here look very different to those higher up.

Vampire squid

Firefly squid **light up** with dazzling blue spots.

Firefly squid

Anglerfish

Glowing in the dark
Many creatures down here make their own light, to attract either prey or mates. This is known as bioluminescence.

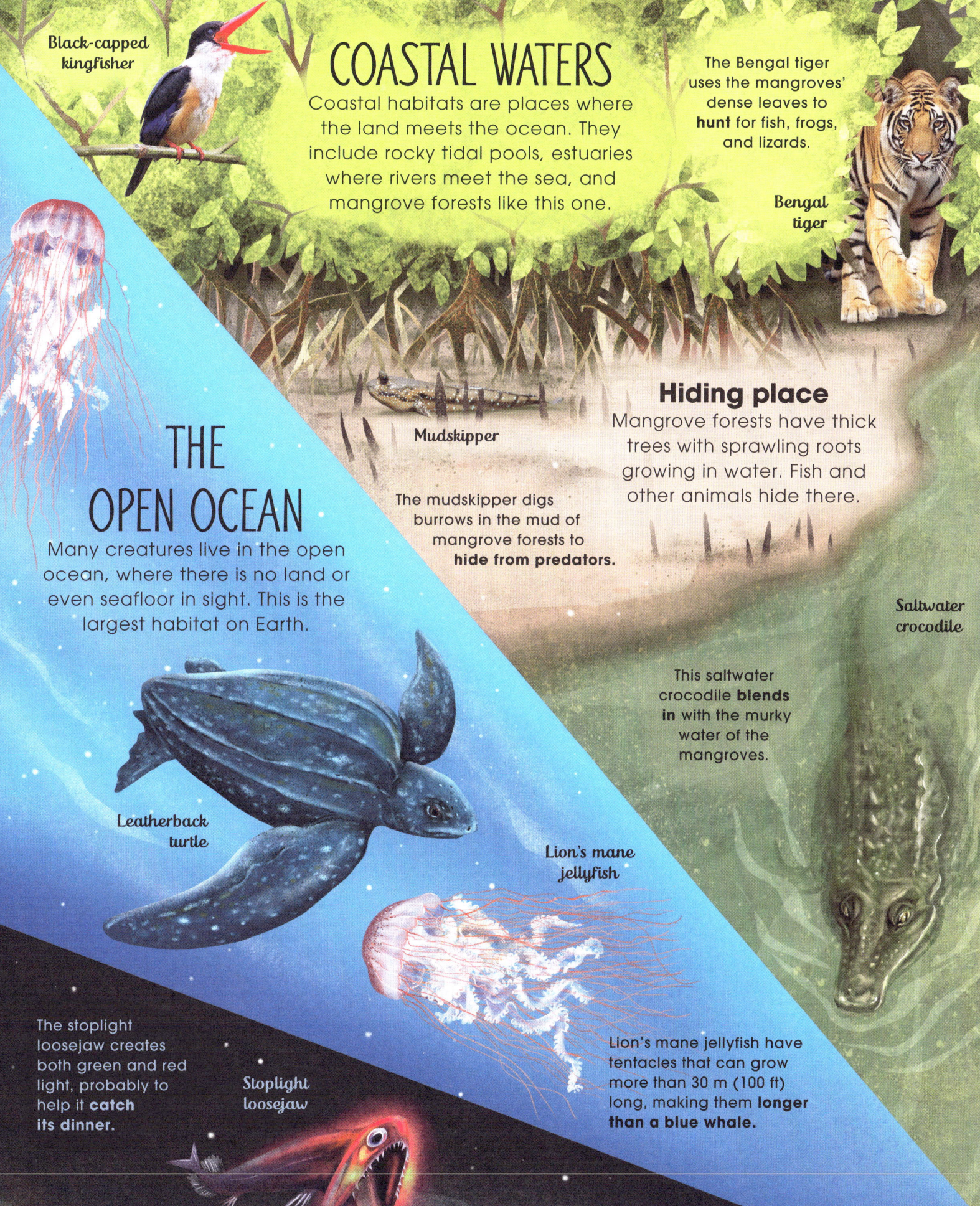

Black-capped kingfisher

COASTAL WATERS
Coastal habitats are places where the land meets the ocean. They include rocky tidal pools, estuaries where rivers meet the sea, and mangrove forests like this one.

The Bengal tiger uses the mangroves' dense leaves to **hunt** for fish, frogs, and lizards.

Bengal tiger

THE OPEN OCEAN
Many creatures live in the open ocean, where there is no land or even seafloor in sight. This is the largest habitat on Earth.

Mudskipper

Hiding place
Mangrove forests have thick trees with sprawling roots growing in water. Fish and other animals hide there.

The mudskipper digs burrows in the mud of mangrove forests to **hide from predators.**

Saltwater crocodile

This saltwater crocodile **blends in** with the murky water of the mangroves.

Leatherback turtle

Lion's mane jellyfish

The stoplight loosejaw creates both green and red light, probably to help it **catch its dinner.**

Stoplight loosejaw

Lion's mane jellyfish have tentacles that can grow more than 30 m (100 ft) long, making them **longer than a blue whale.**

51

Green fingers
Growing your own food is a great way to cut down on waste, save energy, and look after the planet.

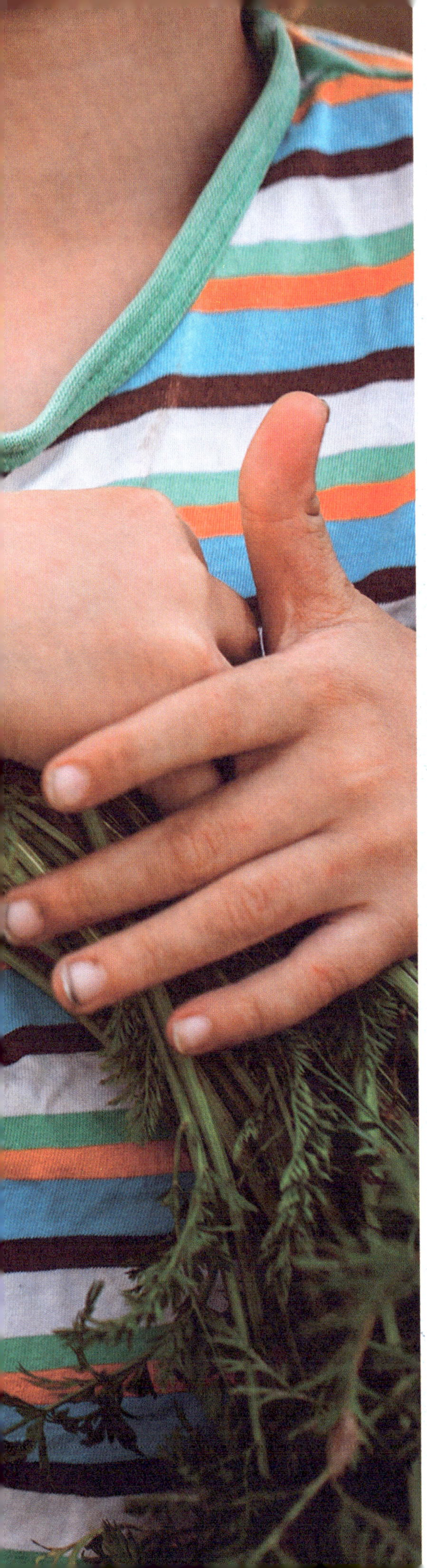

EARTH AND ME

This planet supplies everything humans need to survive – fresh air, clean water, and plenty of plants and animals for food. But with more than 8 billion people on this planet, and the population rising every year, we are starting to stretch the limits of what Earth can provide.

This means that we need to take better care of the planet. Climate change, pollution, deforestation, and overhunting and overfishing are big problems that could spell disaster for all life on Earth.

The good news is that many hardworking people are trying to make sure that Earth stays healthy for centuries to come. **Best of all, you can help!**

Planet in danger

From the clothes we wear and the food we eat to the cars we drive and the houses we live in, everything we do has an impact on our planet's health. Some of our actions are putting our world at great risk.

Animals in danger

Many human activities affect animals. Hunting reduces wild animal populations, and so do habitat loss, lack of food, and pollution.

Amazonian jaguar

Lowland tapir

Amazon River

DEFORESTATION

We cut down forests and use the wood for fuel and building materials. Sometimes the deforested land is turned into farms and towns, removing wild habitats.

Maned sloth

Taking space

Mining, oil and natural gas drilling, and building projects all use space. This pushes wild animals out of their homes, leaving them without shelter and food.

Capybaras

Pollution
Pollution is when harmful substances, such as plastic rubbish or gases and chemicals from factories and cars, are released into the water, air, and soil. This damages habitats and wildlife.

CLIMATE CHANGE
Cutting down trees and burning fossil fuels releases greenhouse gases, especially carbon dioxide, into Earth's atmosphere. These gases make the planet hotter and create all kinds of changes, including wildfires, flooding, melting ice, sea level rises, and extreme weather.

OVERFISHING
High levels of fishing have seriously reduced the world's fish populations. Some types of fish are now struggling to reproduce enough to replace their numbers.

Amazon Rainforest

Brown spider monkey

Helping the Earth

Conservation is what we do to protect our planet. Making changes to how we behave can help us stop more plants and animals from becoming extinct. Here are a few examples of how people are trying to do better.

Sustainable fishing
If we catch wild fish faster than they can reproduce, populations collapse. Laws and restrictions can help keep populations healthy.

Back from the brink
In the 1970s, the Arabian oryx was hunted to near extinction. Today, the wild population is bouncing back thanks to the efforts of conservationists.

Save the whales
Whaling (whale hunting) nearly killed off many species of whales. A global ban was put in place in the 1980s.

SAVE THE ANIMALS!
When a species goes extinct, we lose it forever. To help keep wild animal populations from disappearing, we can use zoo breeding programmes or relocate them to safer habitats.

DO LESS HARM
All over the world, animals are being hunted and killed. Governments can introduce hunting bans and fishing controls to protect wildlife, making sure that it will still be around long into the future.

Protect wildlife
Sometimes wildlife needs guarding. The Maasai Mara National Reserve in Kenya employs park rangers to protect the animals from poachers.

New ways to travel
When exploring natural areas, consider quiet, low-impact ways to get around, such as kayaking, biking, and hiking.

WILDLIFE RESERVES
These protected areas give animals the space they need to live natural lives without the dangers of hunting, poaching, and fishing.

SEE THE WORLD, SAFELY
It's a big world, and there's lots to see and enjoy! Ecotourism is a way visitors can explore places responsibly and the money they spend goes to the local communities.

What can I do?

How can you help the planet? No one person can save the world by themselves, but if we all make just a few small changes, it can add up to make a big impact.

Every little bit
See a sweet wrapper or empty can? Pick it up!

Sort it out
Organize your rubbish and use the right bin for your recycling.

Reusable bag

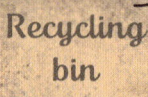

Recycling bin

REDUCE, REUSE, RECYCLE

Every time we buy something new, we use up energy and natural resources, and create pollution. If we reduce the number of products we buy, reuse the ones we have, and recycle when we're done, we can cut down on all three!

Many uses
Reusable bottles can be cleaned and used again for many years.

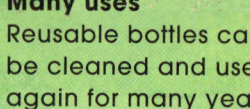

Reusable bottle

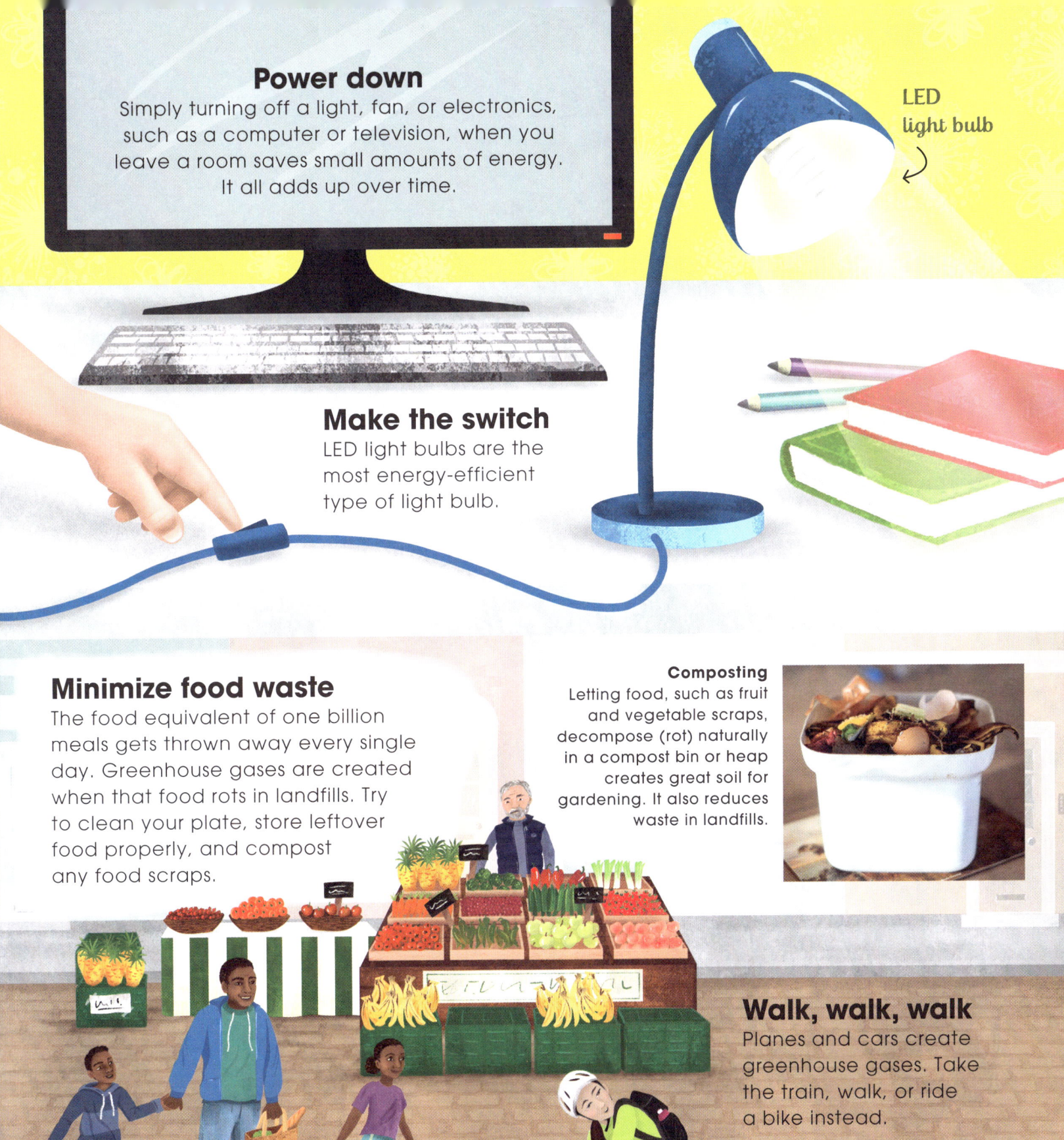

Power down
Simply turning off a light, fan, or electronics, such as a computer or television, when you leave a room saves small amounts of energy. It all adds up over time.

LED light bulb

Make the switch
LED light bulbs are the most energy-efficient type of light bulb.

Minimize food waste
The food equivalent of one billion meals gets thrown away every single day. Greenhouse gases are created when that food rots in landfills. Try to clean your plate, store leftover food properly, and compost any food scraps.

Composting
Letting food, such as fruit and vegetable scraps, decompose (rot) naturally in a compost bin or heap creates great soil for gardening. It also reduces waste in landfills.

Walk, walk, walk
Planes and cars create greenhouse gases. Take the train, walk, or ride a bike instead.

Glossary

ADAPT
How a living thing changes to better survive its environment.

ATMOSPHERE
Layers of gases surrounding Earth.

BURROW
Hole or tunnel dug by an animal.

CAMOUFLAGE
Way of hiding by blending into the colours and patterns of the surroundings.

CLIMATE CHANGE
Changes to Earth's climate over a long period of time, especially due to the release of greenhouse gases, which cause the planet to heat up.

COLD-BLOODED
Animals that cannot regulate their body temperature, so it changes with their environment. These animals often rely on the Sun for warmth.

CONTINENT
Large area of land. Most continents are made up of many countries.

DAM
Barrier designed to hold back water.

DEFORESTATION
Clearing or cutting down of forests.

ELEMENT
Basic substance that contains just one type of atom and cannot be broken down. Elements are the building blocks for everything in the Universe.

EQUATOR
Imaginary line around the middle of Earth that is halfway between the North and South Poles.

FOSSIL FUELS
Natural materials such as coal, oil, and gas that formed underground millions of years ago. Humans burn fossil fuels to make energy.

FRESHWATER
Water that is not salty.

GREENHOUSE GASES
Gases in Earth's atmosphere such as carbon dioxide that trap heat and increase the planet's temperature.

GROUNDWATER
Water that sinks through the ground in spaces between sediment and cracks in rocks.

HABITAT
Natural home or environment of a living thing.

ICE SHEET
Massive and thick layers of compressed ice and snow that cover huge areas of land.

LANDFILL
Place where rubbish and other waste materials are piled up or buried.

LANDSLIDE
When a large amount of earth, rock, and other material move down a slope with tremendous force.

LAVA
Hot, melted rock that comes out of a volcano when it erupts.

MAGMA
Melted rock that is found deep inside Earth.

MAGNITUDE
Measure of how powerful or explosive a volcanic eruption is.

MANGROVE
Trees or shrubs that grow along the coasts of tropical and subtropical oceans. They form mangrove forests.

MIGRATE
Move from one place to another.

MINERAL
Solid, naturally formed substance. Gold, iron, and salt are all minerals.

NORTH POLE
Northernmost point on Earth, located in the Arctic Ocean.

OCEAN SURGE
Change in sea level that is caused by a storm. Ocean surges can lead to flooding.

ORBIT
Path an object takes around another due to gravity, such as how planets go round the Sun.

PERMANENT SNOW
Snow that does not completely melt and stays on the ground year-round.

PLAINS
Area of flat land that very few trees grow on.

POACHING
Illegally catching or hunting wild animals.

PREDATOR
Animal that hunts other animals for food.

PREY
Animal that is hunted by other animals for food.

SALTWATER
Water that contains salt. It is the type of water that is found in seas and oceans.

SAVANNA
Large area of grassland in tropical regions, with few trees.

SOLAR SYSTEM
Collection of objects, such as planets, moons, asteroids, and comets, which orbit the Sun.

SOUTH POLE
Southernmost point on Earth, located in Antarctica.

SUPERHEATED
Liquid that has been heated to a temperature that is higher than its boiling point.

TECTONIC PLATES
Large, slow-moving sections of Earth's surface.

THAW
Ice or snow melting.

THERMOPHILE
Tiny organism that lives in very hot environments.

TROGLOFAUNA
Cave-dwelling animals that have adapted to their dark environment by developing heightened senses of touch, hearing, and smell.

TROPICAL
Something that is related to the two areas near the equator, called the tropics.

TUNDRA
Flat, treeless plains in the Arctic that stay frozen for most of the year.

WARM-BLOODED
Animals that can warm up and cool down their own bodies. Mammals and birds are warm-blooded.

WATERFALL
Area of a river or stream where the water flows over the edge of a cliff or rock and plunges downwards.

WILDFIRE
Huge fires that spread quickly through areas such as forests and grasslands.

Index

Aconcagua, Mount 48
algae 36
Alps 48
altocumulus clouds 17
altostratus clouds 17
amphibians 39
Andes 48
animals 38-51
   in the Antarctic 47
   in the Arctic 46
   in caves 23
   conservation 56-57
   in danger 54
   in deserts 40-41
   extinction 56
   in forests 44-45
   in grasslands 42-43
   in mountains 48-49
   in oceans 50-51
Antarctic 41, 47
Arctic 46
asteroids 6
atmosphere 8-9, 55
auroras 9
autumn 12
axis 10

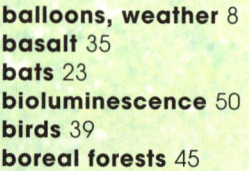

balloons, weather 8
basalt 35
bats 23
bioluminescence 50
birds 39
boreal forests 45

camouflage 41
Cappadocia 26
carbon dioxide 32, 55
caves 15, 22-23
China 34
cirrocumulus clouds 16
cirrostratus clouds 16
cirrus clouds 16
climate change 53, 55
clouds 14-15, 16-17, 20
coastal deserts 41
coastal waters 51
cold deserts 41
comets 6

composting food waste 59
condensation 20
conservation 56
continents 27, 28-29
core 8, 9
crevasses 24
crust 8
cumulonimbus clouds 16
cumulus clouds 17
cyclones 19

day and night 10-11
deep sea animals 50
deforestation 53, 54
deserts 40-41
droughts 18
dwarf planets 6

earthquakes 27, 28, 29, 30-31
echolocation 23
eclipses 11
ecotourism 57
Elbert, Mount 49
electricity 59
energy use 58, 59
epicentre, earthquakes 30
equator 12
eruptions, volcanoes 32
estuaries 51
evaporation 20
Everest, Mount 49
exosphere 9
extinction, life 37, 56

fairy chimneys 26
fault lines, earthquakes 30
fires 18, 55
fish 39
fishing 55, 56
flooding 55
focus, earthquakes 30
food waste 59
forests 44-45, 54
freshwater 20, 21
fumaroles 32, 33
fungi 39

galaxies 7
gases 8, 9, 32
geysers 32, 33
Giant's Causeway 35
glaciers 15, 21, 23, 24-25
Gondwana 29
Grand Canyon 35
Grand Prismatic Spring 33
grasslands 42-43
greenhouse gases 55, 59
groundwater 21

hail 16, 21
heatwaves 18
hibernation 12
Himalayas 49
hot springs 33
humans 38, 53, 54-55
hunting animals 56, 57
hurricanes 19

ice 12, 35
   Arctic and Antarctic 41, 46-47
   in clouds 16
   glaciers 15, 21, 24-25
   ice caves 23
Iceland 33
igneous rocks 34, 35
International Space Station 9
invertebrates 38, 39

krill 47

lakes 21, 35
landfill sites 59
Laurasia 29
lava 32, 34
lava tubes 23
life 5, 6, 37, 38-39
light bulbs 59
lightning 16, 18
light years 7
limestone caves 22
living things 5, 6, 37, 38-39

magma 32, 33, 34
mammals 38
mangrove forests 51

mantle 8
mass extinction events 37
Matterhorn 48
mesosphere 9
metamorphic rocks 34, 35
meteors 9
Milky Way 7
Mojave Desert 40, 41
monsoons 13
Moon 11
moons 6
moraines 25
mountains 28, 48–49

natural resources 58
night and day 10–11
nimbostratus clouds 17
nitrogen 9
North Pole 10, 45
Northern Ireland 35

ocean trenches 28
oceans 4–5
   animals 50–51
   rocks 35
   tsunamis 31
   water cycle 20–21
orbit 10–11
overfishing 55
oxygen 6, 9, 38

Pangaea 29
Panthalassa 29
plants 20, 38, 40, 56
plate boundaries 28
Pluto 6
poaching 57
pollution 53, 55, 58
population growth 53
precipitation 16, 21
predators 42–43, 46

rain 21, 35
   in deserts 40, 41
   monsoons 13
   rainwater 15
   storms 18
rainforests 44

recycling 58
reptiles 38
resources 58
Ring of Fire 29
rivers 21, 35, 51
rock formations 34
rocks 26–27, 34–35
Rocky Mountains 49

saltwater 20, 21
satellites 9
savanna 42–43
sea level rises 55
seasons 12–13
sediment 35
sedimentary rocks 34, 35
seismic waves 31
semiarid deserts 41
sleet 16
sloths 36–37
snow 21
   Arctic and Antarctica 41, 46–47
   clouds 16
   glaciers 24–25
Solar System 6, 7
solfatara 33
South Pole 10
spring 13
stalactites and stalagmites 22
stars 7
storms 18, 19
stratocumulus clouds 17
stratosphere 9
stratus clouds 17
Strokkur geyser 33
sulphur dioxide 32
summer 13
Sun 10–11, 12, 20
sunlight 6, 13, 38, 50
sustainable fishing 56

tectonic plates 27, 28–29, 30, 35, 48
temperate forests 45
temperatures 18
termites 43
thermophiles 33
thermosphere 9
thunderstorms 16, 18

tidal pools 51
tornadoes 16, 19
transpiration 20
travel 57
trees 44–45
Triassic Period 29
troglofauna 23
tropical forests 44
troposphere 8
tsunamis 31
tundra 46
typhoons 19

UFOs 14
Universe 6, 7

valleys 25
vegetables 52
volcanoes 32–33
   rocks 26, 34, 35
   tectonic plates 27, 28–29

walking 59
water 5, 6
   water cycle 15, 20–21
   waterfalls 35
   watering holes 42
   water vapour 16, 20
weather 18–19, 55
weather balloons 8
weathering, rocks 35
whaling 56
wildlife reserves 57
winds 15, 18, 19, 35
winter 12

years 11
Yellowstone 33

Zhangye National Geopark 34
zoos 56

Acknowledgements

The publisher would like to thank the following people for their assistance: Laura Gilbert for proofreading, Hilary Bird for the index, Dheeraj Arora for jacket assistance, and Priya Singh, Ridhima Sikka, and Sakshi Saluja for picture research help.

PICTURE CREDITS

The publisher would like to thank the following for their kind permission to reproduce their photographs: (Key: a-above; b-below/bottom; c-centre; f-far; l-left; r-right; t-top)

1-64 Dreamstime.com: Designprintck (Background texture). **1 Dreamstime.com:** Leklek73 (bl); Simonas Sileika (br); Uvisni (bc); Odze (br/fern). **4-5 Alamy Stock Photo:** Michael S. Nolan. **5 123RF.com:** Oksana Tkachuk (bc); voltan1 (fbr). **Dreamstime.com:** Lee Amery (clb); Steve Mann (bl); N Van D / Nataliavand (br). **7 Shutterstock.com:** NASA images (r). **8 Dreamstime.com:** Okea (br); Staphy (cr). **9 Dreamstime.com:** Andreyi Armiagov (cr). **11 Dreamstime.com:** Valentin M Armianu (br); Daniel Boiteau (cra). **12 Dreamstime.com:** Yuriy Balagula (bl); Jan Rozehnal (c); Harry Collins (cr). **13 123RF.com:** Oksana Tkachuk (Purple cosmos flower); voltan1 (fbr). **Dreamstime.com:** Lee Amery (cb); Ali Nishan (ca); Richard Seeney (c); Anitasstudio (bc); Steve Mann (bc); N Van D / Nataliavand (br/Poppy). **14-15 Getty Images:** Comezora. **16 123RF.com:** bankjayphotto (cl). **Dreamstime.com:** Darinafis (clb/Snow); Flynt (clb/Rain); Justoomm (cb/Sleet). **Shutterstock.com:** Sara Winding (cb). **18 123RF.com:** flower4. **Dreamstime.com:** Iofoto (cra); Sarah2 (ca). **20 Dreamstime.com:** Sergeychernov (cl). **20-21 Dreamstime.com:** Ruslan Nassyrov / Ruslanchik (b). **21 Dreamstime.com:** Pablo Caridad (cra). **22 Alamy Stock Photo:** blickwinkel (cl). **23 Alamy Stock Photo:** Guy Edwardes Photography (bc). **Dorling Kindersley:** Frank Greenaway / Natural History Museum, London (t, t/Bats); Frank Greenaway / Natural History Museum (c). **Dreamstime.com:** Tatiana Belova (cl); Isselee (cb); Glenn Nagel (cra); Mike7777777 (crb). **26-27 Getty Images:** Ron Watts. **29 Dreamstime.com:** Virz87 (bl). **Getty Images / iStock:** Tolga Tezcan (r). **31 Getty Images:** JIJI PRESS (bc). **32 Dreamstime.com:** Sergey Tolmachyov (l). **34 Dreamstime.com:** Atosan (bc); Pannarai Nak-im (c); Vvoevale (cr). **35 Dreamstime.com:** Fokinol (cb); Nicholas Motto (bl); Aitor Muñoz Muñoz (bc). **36-37 naturepl.com:** Klein & Hubert. **38-39 Dreamstime.com:** Odze (b). **38 Dreamstime.com:** Christian Schmalhofer (cr); Leklek73 (bl); Simonas Sileika (br). **Shutterstock.com:** Eric Isselee (c). **39 Alamy Stock Photo:** Bill Gozansky (bl); Nature Photographers Ltd / Paul R. Sterry (br). **Dreamstime.com:** Anankkml (fcr); Irochka (cla); Johannes Gerhardus Swanepoel (ca). **Getty Images / iStock:** izanbar (cra); Tolga Tezcan (tr). **Getty Images:** Jeff R Clow (tc). **40 Dreamstime.com:** Lprovooid (cr). **Getty Images:** Mara Brandl (bl). **40-41 Dreamstime.com:** Ihor Smishko. **41 Depositphotos Inc:** erlantzpererz (cr/coastline). **Dreamstime.com:** Sonya Greer (c/owl); Oleksandr Matsibura (br/Antarctica); Dmitrii Pichugin (tr/African landscape). **Getty Images:** Picture by Tambako the Jaguar (c). **42 Dreamstime.com:** Alexshalamov (cl); Johannes Gerhardus Swanepoel (ca); Stu Porter (c). **43 Dreamstime.com:** Uwe Moser (br); Rixie (tl). **Getty Images:** Nick Dale (c). **44 Adobe Stock:** Lukas (tc/sloth). **Alamy Stock Photo:** Thomas Marent / Minden Pictures (cra/monkey); Luiz Claudio Marigo / Nature Picture Library (cb/capybaras). **45 Dreamstime.com:** Aleksander Bolbot (clb/flycatcher); Iakov Filimonov (c/wolves); Vasiliy Vishnevskiy (tl/woodpecker). **Getty Images / iStock:** Matt Dirksen / E+ (cr/moose); Mark Perry / 500px (c/bear). **46 Alamy Stock Photo:** Michael S. Nolan (tr); Bjørn H Stuedal (cl). **Getty Images:** Dario Maschietti (cb); Paul Souders (cr). **Getty Images / iStock:** Victor Tyakht (br). **47 Alamy Stock Photo:** Auscape International Pty Ltd (bl); piemags / nature (cr); imageBROKER.com GmbH & Co. KG (crb). **Dreamstime.com:** Wedekiba (tr). **Getty Images:** Xavier Hoenner Photography (br). **48 Dreamstime.com:** Anankkml (c); Ondrej Prosicky (clb); Björn Birkhahn (crb); David Havel (bc); Lukas Blazek (tr). **49 Alamy Stock Photo:** Bob Gibbons (bl); Linda Reinink-Smith (cl). **Dreamstime.com:** Bdingman (cb); Isselee (cla); Kerry Hargrove (crb). **naturepl.com:** Gavin Maxwell (cra). **50 Dreamstime.com:** Krzysztof Odziomek (c). **51 Adobe Stock:** robertharding (tr); Tareq (ca). **Dreamstime.com:** Phiphat Suwanmon (tl). **52-53 Dreamstime.com:** Zaikina. **54 Alamy Stock Photo:** Arterra Picture Library / Clement Philippe (cr); Gary Morris Photography (cra). **Dreamstime.com:** Lennyfdzz (bl); Ondrej Prosicky (br). **55 Dreamstime.com:** Lukas Blazek (clb). **56 Depositphotos Inc:** L Peak (cl). **Getty Images / iStock:** Philip Thurston (cr). **57 Dreamstime.com:** Shams Faraz Amir (ca). **59 Getty Images:** Vince Brophy (cr)

Cover images: Front: **123RF.com:** Christopher Fell bl/ (Frog), Mariusz Jurgielewicz tl/ (Flower); **Dreamstime.com:** Robert Hambley bl, Hellmann1 tc, Lori0469 tl/ (bear), Lukas Blazek bc, Shienterprises tl, Rudmer Zwerver bl; **Getty Images / iStock:** Matt Dirksen / E+ cra; Back: **123RF.com:** Mariusz Jurgielewicz tr/ (Flower); **Dreamstime.com:** Robert Hambley br/ (Cardinal), Hellmann1 t, Lori0469 tr/ (bear), Lukas Blazek br, Shienterprises tr, Rudmer Zwerver br/ (otter); **Getty Images / iStock:** Matt Dirksen / E+ br

ABOUT THE AUTHOR

Jason Bittel is a science and wild animal writer from the small town of Acme, Pennsylvania in the USA. He is also the father of three children, as well as one Pomeranian, three hermit crabs, and a garden groundhog named Batman. He thinks science is the coolest and still can't believe he gets to write about it as a grown-up job. Jason is the author of *The Frozen Worlds*, a book in this series, and has written other titles for DK, such as *Mountain*.

ABOUT THE ILLUSTRATOR

Claire McElfatrick is a freelance artist. Her beautiful hand-drawn and collaged illustrations are inspired by her home in rural England. Claire has illustrated all the other books in this series: *The Magic and Mystery of Trees*, *The Book of Brilliant Bugs*, *Earth's Incredible Oceans*, *The Extraordinary World of Birds*, *The Frozen Worlds*, *Prehistoric Worlds*, *The Magic and Mystery of Space*, and *The Magic and Mystery of Earth*.